Dedicated To

My Wife Nandita Sanyal

A Bottle Of Beer and other Poems

Baudelaire II

"You have a Baudelaireian air"

First Published in April 2023

ISBN: 978-93-5741-429-6

BLUEROSE PUBLISHERS
www.BlueRoseONE.com
info@bluerosepublishers.com
+91 8882 898 898

Cover Design:
Aman Sharma

Typographic Design:
Namrata Saini

Distributed by: BlueRose, Amazon, Flipkart

The remark on the outer cover in inverted commas was made by Atul Tiwari (Senior IAS Officer) and I hope I stand true to his remark. Another big compliment I received was from Sir John (Rtd Teacher St. Xavier's School), "Sanyal, one day you will be great." I hope this remark to proves right. As for myself, I chose this title for this book on my humane qualities. The statue on the Front Cover depicts the Old Woman. I hope all of you are moved by the poem.

A line about myself: Presently, I am working in Lalpur Ext. Centre, Birla Institute of Technology, Mesra, Ranchi.

Dr. Balendra Nath Sanyal

Contents

A Flame 1

The Sea 2

Onlookers 3

Healing Touch 6

Journey 7

The Punch Line 8

Rebel 9

The Day You Were Born 10

Stillness 11

Voice of Silence 12

A Careless Game 13

Mischief in The Grave 14

The Tale of A Leaf 15

A Letter to My Girlfriend 18

Tears 22

In the Rains 23

The Ants 26

A Ripple 27

We Meet Again 29

Love 30

The Fern Plant 31

My Pen 32

Present 33

The Epitaph 35

Ecstasy 36

Sunset 37

A Calling 38

Muse 39

Lullaby 40

The Handshake 41

Peter Pan A Mathematical Problem 42

Sacrifice 43

Plunge 44

The Bottle 45

Shadow 46

Memory 47

An Extract from The Parting 48

A Bottle of Beer 50

The Nude Idol 53

Roar Sea 54

A Flame

A night
a candle burns
wavers
shimmers
sometimes
serene.

Molten wax
black wet cotton
lie.

Night
has passed.

The Sea

placid and calm
a picture
Motions play and crawl
in an effort for peace the boat glides on it
the ship moves with weight
the battleship roars
the submarine checks
ducks walk over it
fishes live in it
men live by it
a second world.

Silence moves
the deep secret lies
one picks in a palm
it is mere water
slipping through fingers
or resting in a curve
it seems numb
on some day
she growls
the mute painter draws
the last vestige of love
on one grain
in the vast sea of sands.

Onlookers

Feverish and cold
the things around a stand-still
hot air inside the room
warm water in the bottle
blue chequered shirt
black trousers across the chair
lies in a fixed position
so does the outside
some flowers withstanding heat
old yellow leaves
dirty like the shirt
of a crude shop-keeper
selling oil.
I am in a debt
to these onlookers
starting at me
The crimson face
in a side-street or a lane
I know a duty -
reduce myself to ashes
in that split second
else the face would remain
for ages crimson
I have to pass such exams daily
when I move out

have tea in the nearest shop
sometimes with someone
at times with none
see myself posthumously
take steps like pages in a novel
repeating the movements
protagonists turned old
therefore gold.
old posters across old walls
familiarity breeds contempt
they shall stick for ages
like my memory
pounces on the surest prey
a major historical event
he had never searched
or of a state bread
that makes me remember
in milk it tastes sweet

The story continues
we have a picnic tomorrow
children and perks
sandwiches, soup and cauli-flower
someone will play guitar
my dear friend to relieve
my unusual pain
I will be groaning tomorrow
displaying a crumpled face
reversal of functions
reversal of events
Aristotle gave some name
I shall call it I tried to do it
pondered quite long
it's mighty difficult to find
one is always found out
God catching us
helping a beggar cross the road
and I catch him
awake all-night
or in my dreams while I sleep
why move further
knowing I have been caught
in a trap
by my onlookers
let me dismantle
be another specimen of an ignorant tourist

Healing Touch

Broken bangles scattered
among mud baked walls
The woman in widowhood
picks it gently
one by one
tying in the white cloth
keeps them in the corner
Tomorrow the sweeper
shall sweep them away
along with old newspapers
 having sunday matrimonials.

Journey

Traveller in a moving bus
green fields, farmer and a scarecrow
memory's play turned on
he looks at the conductor
a good fellow, smiles
Main Market, next stop, sir.

Thanks, friend

The Punch Line

The edge of a building in
a canvas
A sure absence
the world breathes in it.

The edge perhaps only
a few dotted lines
a missed line, the lover
desired to speak.

# Rebel

In the glossy silence
of a cold night
the fatigue comes on
residues of experiments
falls and sticks
a network of lines
a fragmented canvas
the crack extends
the broken lines of a palm

The Day You Were Born

Catch the reins of horror
with the strength of earth
in on your ten fingers
cover your face in perpetual darkness
in those strong fingers
the brightest vision looms
heralding the night
you were about to be born.

Stillness

a quiet beauty
drops of rain
on grey brown patch of land.
Moments later, children
play marbles.
a marble-in blue, green and red
shines in a holy position.
children-smiles flicker on colourful shirts.
rainbow stays on my earth
- a patch thirty meters wide
beside the house where I stay
let us, bigger children,
my elders, bigger children than me,
come out and stand together solemnly
to take a deep breath
The rainbow, rises, but
before I tell you how it looks.
it has risen a few feet up
It is ephemeral
in the stillness of a breath
I see another rising.

Voice of Silence

is a grave
the field through the angled window
the glass pane dances
the tall eucalyptus
tries to tear its leaves
Cannot.

The grave
the dead leaves
on a paper
recurring decimals
another leaf falls
a decimal is added.

An open book
the recurr' smiles
a page falls on other
in a graveyard.
one dissolves, other emerges
a broom never lies
in a graveyard.

A Careless Game

Squeezing of an insect
is never painful
it happens
the insect dies
in the palms are tiny specks
of mortality.

Death is an insect
it crawls over the bed sheets
moves under the slippers
cries when unnoticed
touch, care, fondle or stamp
a speck shall always fall.

Mischief in The Grave

From the graves
one hears death
speaking the body in a compact coffin
moments before
in continuous moments moving back
it had spoken
now, it speaks.

A glow
- eyes, skin, veins
out of the coffin
cries and laughs
the game begins.

He shall play
a longer game
which he had played
a moment ago.

The Tale of A Leaf

I
Between the limbs of the trees
a hazy halo lies still
illuminating the leaves
looking at heaven.

II
The air blows
brothers and sisters together
in murmurous whispers warn themselves
on their existence.

Precariously they had stood
huddled together in confusion
clinging to each other
embracing in honest fear.

A rustle in the air
-a nod at a dark desolate place
a suspicious opening of a door
the visitor goes unnoticed, unfelt.

Many cold winters
many died in a sweep
others brought down in a hard struggle
warriors - a spine firmly implanted
limbs exterminated.

Few still live
the victors - the flapping flags

the losers - the wind smiles on them
broken nutshells of a one sided match.

III
Another birth
an odd one
silent, calm, lone
existing in a world of its own.
In the night his life began
amidst the hushed silence
the slightest quiver, the remotest echo
fell upon the throbbing vein.
A new life
the off-spring of
sighs, tears, rage, madness
emblem of emancipation.

IV
After days of lull
a spark, a tremor, a forewarning
impulsively the wind set forth
on the path of destruction.
The tree scared
waved, a hapless state
the brave little one
amusingly stood erect.
The wind burst out
the young general stepped
out a determined calm radiated
every leaf glowed in its abundance.
A single breath was heard
a mysterious unifying force

a deep seething rage expressed
an unquenched fervour of ages.

The commander brandished his sword
thousands followed the warrior
a shrieking cry was heard far and near
the wind had been struck.

The heavens poured out in glee
happily the leaves wept
to the benefactor they looked
a laughing waving leaf.

V

He is at the apex
the brightest child of the old mother
adorning the mother
green, full green is she.

A Letter to My Girlfriend

ASPIRATION I

In the silence
of my room
i soak my head
in the bucket full of water
and water dripping
covered by a towel
i play music
i write a letter
i write the truth
and feel good
the letter dangles from pocket
a thin blue jutting out
from chequered green
and go to post it eagerly
carefully take it out
smooth it twice
read the name again carefully
darken the first letter
to express my sincerity
and finally roll it in
somehow there is no voice

has it lost itself
i again stroke the entire apparatus
the gurgling sound
i feel myself comfortable
my thoughts have settled itself
in the bottom layer
safe and sound.

REJUVENATION II

I remember
a cricket match
i played badly
no excuses for that
preoccupied i had soaked
my head, already said before
but somehow now i remember
water had entered my nostrils
now, i have itching sensation
i have determination
to remove my past performance
to remove the moistened dust
of my troubled nose
i talk to my friends
i talk about the letter
i talk it is beautiful
they say that i am self praising
they speak of envy
they write letters out of habit
i wrote because i had to
i wrote because my fingers itched
i wrote because i saw
my veins quivering.

NUMBNESS III

The blue square rests
i rest too
i am tired
my breath appears as a stranger
i get thrilled
to see me panting
to see me gulping down air
i give a big laugh
i joke on myself
i play with thousands of my beings
they are all so fun-loving they fiddle on my armpits
i am a big elephant
squirrels and ants run over me.

Tears

you unfold
like a boy cheating
from neighbour
ready not to be caught
yet helplessly uncontrollable.

In the Rains

I

Locked in the room
a smell of wet clothes
hangs on to my nostrils
packet of cigarettes
lie on my table
envelopes of little use
until mind gets numb
one practises love making
writes some beautiful lines
reads it once, twice, not more
the cigarette and the envelope
idle passengers, closer while it rains.
I cannot bathe in rains
why can't I
with my trousers
rolled walk in the path alone.

II

Little plants turned bright green
trees with a load of water
pigeons partly wet
the balcony flutters
on their winged sound
the world breathes outside
I,
unable to decide
where I belong
step outside
get wet, hair parted
to touch life
when most unprepared
falling on a pebble.

III

Who calls me
by my name
in the solitary walk
on a street barren of desire?
to the posthumous room
where game of life is played without result?
Who is the messenger
when I expect none
and conveys words
which glide past me?
Shall I receive or give?

IV

The stink of the room
has not abated
the night hops and jumps
seeks grain in hunger
bits and pieces it collects
from unrolled sheets
fades away just past
probably to my friend's room
and play another game
of hide and seek.

V

I cannot absolve
of my numbness
grown with the still water
circular brown rings
stilted immobile past
The future-

a magic wand
displayed aong the crowd
we hold our breath or gasp in wonder
the ring stretches
I wait for the unseen hand.

The Ants

Restless souls on my roof's black green holes
Small delightful, moving, destination unknown
never tired, all alone

Their curiosity, their beauty
make me mighty
I feel Almighty.

A Ripple

A ripple quivers
carried in soft breathes
like a young dream moving
A self-contended man with a cigarette
across a street full of people
caring not to brush his pressed shirt.

He moves to a prostitute's home
the winding ways disturb him not
few hairs of his head
scattered by the directionless air
the bootlaces drop from his shoe
tucked under the sox,
above the sole.

Knocks the large door
of countless waves gossiping
the waves open the door
the stranger motionless stands
some play upon his feet
others let their terraces fall.

He lies in the light of midnight
in the bed of thousand spasms
climbs over aimlessly
reaches upon the surging belly
rolls over in animated fury
Falls.

We Meet Again

First of January
- a drop of water
quivering, expecting, cherishing
and breaks.....

The broken fragments lie scattered
in the remaining days
we pick them up accidentally
across unknown paths and lanes

Every man carries others fragments
we meet to reaffirm
it's death within ourselves
It's continuity in other's soil.

A little red flower woke up
from the cushioned bed of green
looked at the soft blue sky
and said 'Love'.

The Fern Plant

The fern plant lay in one corner
gay, pretty and smiling
sheltered by two huge rocks
a child of ageless parents

Two human eyes fell
upon the merry soul
how sweet how tender!
they gleefully cried

She would be in our garden
she would be watered
she would be our little friend
they poured in joy

She was plucked
meekly she rests in their palms
the playful child
in their arms.

My Pen

is but a stroke of chance
caught in a shop
lying idly with others
i put my signature
and she became mine.

 Present

My wearied soul complained
like a bare child crying.
She is always at pain
at the slightest hurt
and hankers always for a gift.

I gave her a simple toy.
She burst out in laughter.
I looked at her helplessly
knowing no other present
on bereft paying dunes.

I wandered
across the sands alone
watching the ripples play
moisten the sands
a child

A voice spoke
very near to me
as a long lost friend
"stroke the ripples by your fingers
see the play of doll".

The saddest picture
a doll playing
the sweetest picture
a doll playing
the barest present a doll playing.

The Epitaph

Ruined walls
by a countryside lake
the water is still
autumn leaves lie on it
swans in sleep

A traveller reaches
tries to write a few lines
not a word is written
blank space

Ecstasy

To be;
with a five year old child
in thoughts
and joy
a school girl before god.

How lonesome the looks
amidst a hundred praying
with closed eyes and folded hands.

Five year old
believe me it is not brotherly
i pine most seriously
Passion to touch -
and burn in a mysterious fire.

Sunset

A little boy walked past me
I called him-Hey
TO watch the sunset?
How does it look my friend?
Red,l very red, I see it daily,
you are alone?

I have to slip from my home
I have to get away from my friends
What do you do there?
I sit and sit and sit
I talk and talk and talk
I laugh and laugh and laugh
Alone?

Everybody is with me
They also talk, laugh and play
What does the sun do?
The sun watches the play
forgets to close his eyes
though I know it is night

A Calling

To Nina Singh

From unknown origin
a pain is felt
and gradually settles down
to every cell of my being
a panting search
but no reason express the delicate torture
softly pouring from the mournful eye
and gently consoled on a blank page.

Muse

How often you come to me
when i silently wait
to envelop in your shade

you pass by me silently
as a careless lover i let you pass
you move away in a corner and speak

the first word of my first line
my hands tremble to put you down
i fear to kiss you

Messenger sober me down
let me be a being.

Lullaby

You might have heard
some died of love
Suicides
How about this one?
Moments elapse
he caught one of the commonest disease
cold, cough, toothache or slight pain
and he died
The body did not
want to live
so he died
a simple death
more easy than killing
a mosquito with slap
the others
never heard of this death
consumed indifferently by life.
no mosque, coffin or pyres
a tale told by grandmaa
to make the young child sleep

The Handshake

In a movie
a young lady with wrinkles
scattered on her temples
extended her hands
to the young man
Moments elapsed
eternity passed
between the fingers
from somewhere a voice rang
Beautiful.

The man surely had heard
the single voice
He sought for a lone help
hoping to meet the void.
His impatience grew
the confidence fell
rings of anger drawn on his face
soon enveloped by a chill
a face of loosing memory
before an exam

Peter Pan A Mathematical Problem

grows beneath the soil

a potato

fastened to a corner

a point

to form a square or triangle

that brings us

taught in schools

one free

the other in chains

how do we choose?

brothers, sister, mothers, fathers, beloveds

answer me

two-fifths of one, three-fifths of other

wonderful artistry

did my beloved say

zero and one?

the stunted growth

of my protaganist

and reads Eucleid

to understand a point

and love me.

Sacrifice

The queen was struck
within a few minutes of the match
the smaller ones were engaging themselves
pawn, pawn, pawn, pawn, knights, bishops, rooks
huddling together in front of their king
vulnerability a forte
a pawn thrusts itself
a sacrificial lamb
lives in the centre
who holds him?
Cynical smile
in the opposition
the small fellow
knocked off
Betrayal: betray
lies dead with Queen
One in battle
one in gaining honour
gatecrashing immortality.

Plunge

The boy looks at the fan
lying still
takes a ladder
clings to the rod
stop there for quite sometime
his hands perspire
he falls down
Swings round and round in the floor
his nose takes a circular turn
his eyes bulge and depress
washes his face-tries to
water gets stuck on his face
tries to rub it off
it slips through his fingers
puts his head straight into
a bucketful of water
feels his hair twine and twine
a long column of hair
bubbles clutch on
the each streak rubs on to the other
the familiar turns
of everyday life
zig-zag puzzles hold on to each other
a beautiful cross word formed
the answer will be given tomorrow.

The Bottle

The empty bottle, upside down
placed on the cup, straight
standing erect
on the brink of existence

No one wonders
all securely placed
dead leaves on dead lanes
waiting to be buried
entered in dust-bins

Among thousand such spectators
among the drinking group in a room
in the dead frenzy of stilted shouts
and foolish Wah, Wah's
the bottle only stands
the.

Shadow

A voice disturbs me
I try a cruel act
to check the tear
- the love of time
when it moves in setting sun.

The restrain to prevent
loving the i within me
The bounteous drop
cringes and chokes
and dies.
It has never made love
with the burning cheek.

I call myself
in whispers and soft tone
in harsh and cracking noise
believing that time
shall stop to hear me
and I shall look larger
than I am.

Memory

pale purple night
you throttle breath
each one a gasp a cry
aloud in night
barer and barer
passionately undressing
the shame, guilt, horror
of being tortured
without a resistance

Creature,
what is your history?
continuous unfolding of laps
Death to beginning
End to life
I drown you
the unfaithful echo.

An Extract from The Parting

To Bindu Godara.

The woman stood
the man spoke
his last words
"Bye, if ever we meet
have a good laugh at chance".

The woman trembled the man dissolved
into the night
not a trace left
a lost person.

The woman gazed
no man was there
trees, trees, trees,
leaves, leaves, leaves,
roots, roots, roots:

The woman saw
the image of man
clear, lucid, jovial
stuck, rooted, grounded
in the film of a long silent tear.

A Bottle of Beer

Two good friends sat in a hotel
with a bottle of beer
to ease away some time
and mutually rejoice.

One was a good listener
the other a tale-teller
the two watching each other
in silent affection.

Softly poured a quote
'Nihil humani a le alienum puto'
Embarrassingly he tried to explain
Every man I try to love.

"Everybody does," the indifferent reply,
the teller not dismayed
his eyes gleamed clear
a big gulp of beer.

There was an old woman
the Over-Bridge being her shelter
she lay there motionless
watching the strangers pass.

Known by all was she
her name called - Maa-Jee
nobody gave her money
all offered her in kind.

The school boy running across
the youth with a buoyant air
the elderly, an affected grimness
a smiling recipient to all.

The listener absently requested.
Another bottle or two!
Looked at his friend
whose eyes-a bright light

Withering old age
and she fell ill
slept with a chaddar over her
in the street

Dust rolled over
insects ran on the body
an uncared thing she lay
rewarded, not termed a beggar

The listener cried aloud
'why was she not taken to hospital?
why not provided a doctor?
why this bastardly act?'

The teller sensed his victory
cautiously he replied
'she could not receive
the bounties of human love'

The listener lay defeated
the teller in complete triumph
the fan moving
the hotel bare

One last question 'you loved her?'
a tear silently rolled
the listener looked at the victor
'oh! This true tale just for a bottle of beer!

The Nude Idol

The startleness of nudity
The crippled soldier
in a field operation
bullets spray around
the venom somewhere is lost
and yet he waits for the death
the curves; big as blotches of blood

A naked woman wailing
each part a layout
for the inevitable
the desire to the desireless
that creeps and clings
the stairs of purposelessness
again tiny blotched but of brown
lack of potassium and nitrate
on a leaf
the loss, injustice
that lingers on to
then stops with a thud, killing one.

Roar Sea

Entirely separate worlds
The day and night, by the sea
From a balcony

You see the white foams
Rushing in spectacularly
From the middle

Some gathering momentum
Till it reaches the shore
And a calm resides

Not so in the night
Where the blackness of sea
Unfathomable, impenetrable and roaring

While Mozart in the twinkling waters
What our eyes see and mind fathoms
The blackness and enormity of the sea Beethoven.

A darkness, vivd and illuminating
Only to the ears
Where a deaf sea ever hear

Roar harder Sea
For Beethoven has gone deaf
Let him hear his own music